Membrane Towers

Lin West

First published in 2021 by Paragon Publishing, Rothersthorpe

ISBN 978-1-78222-888-2

Book design, layout and production management by Into Print
www.intoprint.net
+44 (0)1604 832149

To

Chris, Ivy and Patrick, Children, Grandchildren
and Great Grandchildren – love as always

CONTENTS

FOREWORD

I have been familiar with Lin West's poetry for some years now, mostly poems about her life experiences and her family and friends, but it wasn't until I took on the role of editor of the *Eastry Village News* that I fully appreciated her talent.

Each issue I ask her to submit a poem or two to be included in the magazine and each time I get exactly what I want with no fuss and no changes or correction needed. More recently I have asked her to write poems on specific subjects – lockdown, coming out of lockdown, Remembrance Sunday, Anti-social behaviour and Health matters to name a few. However, the one that will always stick in my mind is the poem she did about the life of Captain John Harvey, an 18th century naval hero who lived in the village – in this she truly surpassed herself.

Lin writes from the heart. There is a simple honesty to her poetry that we can all associate with and she uses all her life experiences to the full in her subject matter and is certainly not one to beat about the bush. She loves writing and puts heart and soul into everything she does. A rare talent indeed!

Patrick Clarke

MEMBRANE TOWERS

Sometime in the nineties

Then, when fingers grated through endless chores and
every day seemed like Monday, she longed for passing showers
Whilst babies slept and floors were swept,
she'd write in membrane towers
To anyone else they wouldn't make sense,
her collection of coloured ink
A catalogue of the day's events, stacked by the kitchen sink

From years seventy one to ninety two, she kept her heart-line
flowing
P.T.O'S and "watch this space" proud memories slowly growing
Stories of teeth, and scribbled lines, pages crammed with
laughter
Photographs of self-respect, remembered ever after...

Structured rules, a balanced cost, what price for independence,
A stolen curl of feather down, still stroked with fond
remembrance
Indoor picnics without bees, and hats of shiny paper
Scuffed shoes, and grazed knees, the famous egg hunt caper

Let's pretend and make believe, alive between the pages
Precious times of years gone by preserved for future ages.
Weeks and months of growing pains, and chapters full of
learning
Dignity and discipline, and cogs slowly turning
So that was then when nappies dried, between the passing
showers
Allowing her the stolen time to write the Membrane Towers.

Alternative Humour

A TEST FOR OLD WRINKLIES

Here is a quiz so do as you are told,
Answer all questions and lo and behold,
If you answer correctly a prize you will win
A disguise for your birthday my dear friend Lyn.

The first thing to do is poke out your tongue,
Come on now no cheating, it has to be done.
If it's pink and not furry your scores not begun
If it's rough and insipid you start with a 1

Now for your eyes are they clear crystal blue
Or bloodshot and cloudy, if so notch up 2
Do you hunt for your glasses therefore to see?
A yes puts your score, quite firmly on 3

You're doing so well you're very nearly there
Next for a question concerning the chair...
Early evening after work, do its comfort you seek
Then ten minutes later have you fallen asleep?

A predictable answer, are you quite sure?
Well done! You old snorer you're safely on 4
There's just one more answer and it's worth a good 5
Remember back-combing, stilettos, the jive?

You do... what a marvel; you've finally struck gold,
It's official, I mean it, you're now really old!
So what have you won for completing this task?
Don't you know clever arse, of course it's a mask!

ANTISOCIAL BEHAVIOUR

There's a ton of Ants marauding like an army,
Thundering past me ever so calmly!
Not thinking or caring, I could wipe them out,
With hot water and bleach poured through a spout.

What gives me the right to end their strife?
Play judge and jury, to end their life.
I call myself civilised, empathic and fair
 Not according to the ant washed out there!

I need to take heed for we need our Ants,
To aerate the soil and oxygenate plants.
We can't live without them this is so true,
They're crucial and important, clever too!

They outnumber us easily, 1.5 million to one,
A fact we ignore as the deed it is done!
And yet, just think if they turned on us
It wouldn't' be a splash, more like a bus

Flattening us savagely as we have done them
Acting triumphantly, their time has come
For Ant's rights matter no more drowning out
Their place in this world, needed beyond any doubt!

BORN LUCKY

Some of us are born lucky
With nothing much to do
Then others are just overworked
The kind like me and you
We rise at dawn to face the day
And earn our daily bread
Then wonder why we wasn't born
A lucky one instead!

INAPPROPRIATE

Every so often, well, once in a while,
I get the feeling I need to smile
I'll be sitting in the car and I'll stop at the lights,
A hearse to the left, an ambulance to the right.
Then it will appear without any warning
I'm sitting smiling at people in mourning.

EGGIE HUNT

I don't think I'll find them, but I'm still prepared to look
I won't give up too easily I'll search in every nook
I've been to all the places where I usually get my fix
I like to have a dozen but I'll make do with six

If I can't find my large ones, small ones will do
If push comes to shove, I'll share a box with you
Chicken is my favourite, but Goose will suffice
In this time of "Lockdown" we will pay the price.

Seeing my box empty, oh how I cried
No more scrambled "eggies," omelette, or fried
I can't give up my "eggies," but the soldiers can go
Oh to taste my "eggy bread", I do miss you so

I need some really quickly; I won't give up my fight
Brown is my preference, but I'll settle for white
So if anyone is reading and takes pity with my plea
Please pop round later, I'll have poached egg for tea.

FRIENDS LAUGHING OVER TEA

I wouldn't let the day go by, without a certain little mention,
Of how we use to be when young, always leading to detention!
The famous five had nothing on us as we lived and mocked society
We never did what we were told as we lived without sobriety!
Yes, life for us was just a game, of hitch-hikes, laughs, and tricks
Not forgetting a few boys of course to add into the mix!
A motley crew if ever there was, distinct from others we knew,
Sometimes known as bullies, this of course was just not true!
Just young girls quite easily led, all family and friends together
A special friendship bond, memories lasting forever.
Ches was the smallest, with her body lean and slight
We used her as Guy Fawkes, collecting for bonfire night.
Of course that's not all she did, she was good at telling lies
Like her uncle who lived in the windmill, nothing but porky pies.
However Ches that was long ago, Just a memory we all share
Like false teeth and wrinkles, and faces full of hair.
Talking of hair I think of Dee and how she trimmed our locks
Cut our hair in the legion, as I knitted the coloured socks
We all had matching jumpers; we thought we were the elite
Crochet dresses, army coats, Doctor Martins on our feet.
And who remembers cross country, sweating buckets back in the days
The saving grace for us was good old *"Listways."*
Bena and Mary's home of course, as we skipped from field to fag
Whilst others carried on running, we had it in the bag!
Talking of fags I still see her now, as she emerges soaking wet
Poor old Bena fell in the pond, but still she did not fret.
Just stood there sucking frantically, to keep her dog end alight
It gave us a good old laugh, poor Bena a nasty fright!

Christine was the defender, she didn't suffer fools gladly
And Chippy our little peacemaker, no longer with us sadly
Mitch was the joker, we all remember that crazy smile
And Mary silent but stoic, eyelashes, long, to beguile.
Sue and Jack were our runners, had legs like a fine gazelle
God help anyone who passed them, they sure would give them hell!
Memories that never fade away, bring nostalgia to the fore,
Drinking beer and having fun smooching on the *"Rat ole"* floor.
Dancing round our handbags, we were a sight to see
Young, excited and happy, 60's children reckless and free
Such happy times of days gone by no longer within our reach,
Like home perms, ten bob notes and trips to Margate beach!
Remember girls on Gillies bus, to the sea we would descend
Visit Dreamland in its glory, a whole five bob to spend!
Oh the sheer pleasure as we screamed from ride to ride
Our mams playing Bingo, our dads drunk at their sides
We wore cardboard in our daps, used chalk to make them white
Saggy swimming costumes, we looked an awful sight!
Oh such lovely memories of our lives I now have told
Never thinking that the time would come
when we would get so old
Nevertheless our minds are the same, spirited feisty and free
Recalling our precious memories with *"Friends Laughing over Tea"*

NEGATIVE DAY

Shall I bake a cake?
I haven't an egg.
Shall I take a walk?
I would but my leg...
Shall I read a story?
I've finished my book
Perhaps play Chess
I misplaced the Rook
What would I like to do?
To pass the time
Sit here scribbling nonsensical rhyme.

OUT OF TUNE

A tune of semiquavers,
Quivered to the Clef
Please help us find our places
E.G.B.D.F

DATING BY NUMBERS

D.t to D.t people positioned in the room,
A match made in heaven you'd naturally assume.
1. Joined to 2.. and 2 joined to 3...
3... joined to 4.... and 4.... Joined to me.
The picture formed quite quickly
A bed of roses took its shape,
Divorce happened suddenly,
When 10..........rubbed out 8........
My join with 6...... was cancelled
and 7.......was in doubt,
9......... teethered anxiously,
It was time for me to shout!
I may only be a number,
But I deserve to challenge fate
Reshaping the whole outline,
9........ Joined with 8........
Fate shifted the dynamics,
 And 10..........rejoined 11...........
I rejoined 6...... and 6 rescued 7.......
The sequence seemed quite logical
Wouldn't you agree?
Then why oh, why for heaven's sake,
Did 12...........join with me?"

SNOW SLIP

Like icing sugar on a chocolate cake,
The garden was covered by dawn.
A thick white coat, so clean and crisp,
Had frozen the garden lawn
I ran towards the cupboard,
Pulled on my hat and coat,
Then grabbed a pointy carrot,
And a scarf for round his throat
Meticulously I built my man
Used currants for his eyes
Then ran and poised my camera
To share my handsome prize
But as I pressed to "send" him
I slipped and knocked his head
And Instead of sharing his photo
I'd flattened him instead.

MONEY TRAP

Money is useful, but it can't buy health
Just another label, we know it as wealth
Well "wealth" can be fleeting, at times surreal
Useful for spending and making the steal
To have it feels powerful, invincible, and strong
Like a choir of angels, united in song
We use it to bargain and validate our name
Be someone important head of the game
And yet when we're done, on the final call
We realise, quite simply it's no use at all.

THE SHOPPING TROLLEY

How does it happen?
I'm sure it knows I'm there
Drawn to it like a magnet
Hypnotised by its steely glare
I really blame myself
Should shove it back in the pile
Instead of acting like a bronco
trying to tame it up the aisle!
I feel as though it's laughing
On some huge ego trip
Waiting for me to flounder
Bringing an end to my shopping trip
But I persevere regardless
Fill my carriers to their peak
Then hurry to the car park
Leaving my monster for another week!

WRINKLES

What can I do there's no turning back,
Things are getting tricky, they're waiting to attack!
Creeping on my flesh, they make their mark
I think I will look better, sitting in the dark!
It started with a couple underneath the eyes
They won't go away, no matter how I try.
Long slimy feet etching in my skin
Changing all my features...the rot's setting in!
How can I fight them, without looking ill
Plaster on the face cream, swallow another pill.
Go to the Chemist search through every shelf,
Time is of an essence so care for yourself.
No one can evade them, wrinkles will prevail
But this is not the end of my familiar tale.
I have a solution, so everyone take heed,
Wrinkles will be banished women will be freed.
Just walk past every mirror, and surely you will see
That beauty is on the inside, ah, well it worked for me!

THE GRIM REAPER

When death comes knocking and it's our time to go
Will we fight on say definitely "no"
Or will we give in say a gracious "yes"
Welcome the peace... a time to undress
Accept our fate give one last sigh
The end of the script for both you and I
Or will we fight on like some huge Oak
Stoic and fierce, refuse to be coke
Ashes and dust is not our style
We'll rebel and shout... "Leave us for a while"
Come back next year, we're not ready to go
When we're ready, no fear, you'll be the first to know!

WHAT TO DO

I could learn to paint, like Constable or Turner,
Or take up comedy and become a Gurner!
I could learn to juggle, with knives or spears,
Thinking about it I've juggled for years.
I could learn to speak French, Parle vous Francais
Knit jumpers and hats, go out for the day
It all seems quite tangible, just need to choose one
But sadly I'll be doing nothing, for the whole day is done!

REVENGE IS SWEET

The doors of the hall flew open, as she floated in lamppost high
In her arms she carried a poodle, a rue twinkle in her eye
Around her neck she wore her memories, bleached curls
adorned her head
Her scarlet lips were tainted, with words she'd left unsaid
The haunting apparition, sent shivers through the room
Gasps of "oh dear it can't be" echoed loudly through the gloom!
Her presence hailed a silence, as though she were a saint
She eyed her bullies squarely, and then savoured every faint!

LOTTERY HEAVEN

All five numbers and a bonus ball off seven...
I've just gone and won my lottery heaven...
Not going to save it...and yes hell, it will change my life
 I'm going on the internet to buy myself a wife...

Going to buy myself a big mac, going to by myself some shoes,
No more dodging puddles or fighting for yesterday news.
No more buskers belly rumbling whilst I sleep,
Cos I've gone and hit the big time...going to have dry feet...
la la...gonna eat

All five numbers and a bonus ball of seven,
just gone and won my lottery heaven
It will change my life...say goodbye to strife...
it will change my life la la la

No more sleeping with one eye open,
no more second hand food
Cos I've gone and hit the big one going to be a rich old dude
Hell yes it's going to change me, I'm going to be a star
I'm going to be a star be a star...la la la...yes a star

Christmas

1950'S CHRISTMAS MEMORIES

A tired old fairy in a crumpled dress
Sits at the top of the tree no less
With its thread bare branches, faded green
Balanced on the telly, still looks serene

A dancing father Christmas, older than me
Creaks and groans, with an arthritic knee
Tattered old paper chains, faded and torn
Hang from the ceiling, looking rather worn

A yellowing card, with a faded red bow
Sitting on the Mantel. Oh! So long ago
Christmas memorabilia cherished and loved
By a fifties child, who lived, laughed and loved
CHRISTMAS.

CHRISTMAS IS CANCELLED

Christmas Eve, started fine, all was merry and bright
The fairy was in her usual place, not a problem seemed in sight!
The Elves were packing the surprises for every girl and boy
And filling up the Christmas sacks for everyone to enjoy!

There didn't seem an issue; in fact what could go wrong
Santa's done this many times, singing the reindeer song
But this year it seems different, something not quite right
In fact for dear old Santa, it was the beginning of his plight

There's going to be no Christmas, it's cancelled now for sure
No more climbing down chimneys or presents on the floor
But Santa's sleigh is gleaming, reindeers sanitised and clean
Waiting for their leader who's red nose, could not be seen!

So Santa now is worried, it's never happened before
He'd need to go and investigate, wearing his mask for sure!
And then that's when he saw him, looking sad but so serene
Poor old Rudolf's caught the virus, and is stuck in quarantine!

CHRISTMAS

Well it's almost here this festive thing
With baubles and bangles and bells that ring
Out with the old in with the new
Cakes to bake and planning to do
A tree to dress a turkey to stuff
Presents to buy there's never enough
Mince pies and pickles, sausage rolls and beer
A recipe designed to add some cheer
So bring it on this festive thing
For it's Christmas time ding a ling ding.

EVE OF CHRISTMAS

It's the Eve of Christmas; I'm trying to sleep,
I've read my books, and counted sheep.
Under the blankets, I mustn't look;
My stocking's hung upon the hook.

In walks Mum, out of the gloom,
"Close your eyes, he'll be here soon."
My heart's pumping, my adrenalin's high,
I feel so anxious, I almost cry.

Where's the sleep fairy, is she in bed,
Forgotten me now, oh what dread!
What if I see him, and he disappears,
Forgetting my bike, I've waited for years!

Miss all the sweets, goodies and pop,
I'll spoil it all, an empty sock!
I'll take my punishment, nothing for me;
Console myself, dripping for tea!

Then in walks Mum, "wake up, he's been,"
The fattest sock I've ever seen.
A brand new bike, a "Raleigh" for sure,
A wish come true, on foot no more.

Proud as punch, I couldn't be better;
Good old Santa read my letter!
How lucky am I not to be missed,
And I also dreamt he gave me a kiss!

LIN'S MEMORIES OF CHRISTMAS PAST

There's something about the season, evoking memories for me
The smell of peeling a tangerine, placing baubles on the tree
Filling up the hamper box, like Magpies with their loot
Eating sugared almonds and endless tins of fruit!
Saving to buy the turkey, hung on the back of the door
Nothing wrapped in plastic, always fresh for sure
Relishing the roasted nuts, trifle, meat and cheese
Singing well known Carols whilst feeling calm, at ease
Cards pegged like washing on string around the room
Candles in the window fading far too soon
Oh such lovely memories, of a time gone by
Nostalgic, Christmas past, diamonds in the sky.

Love and Emotion

MY DAD AND I

My Dad and I would always go
To Kearsney Abbey, we loved it so
He in his suit and me in my dress
Which Mum had made for Sunday best
Swaggering along one hand in his pocket
He'd buy me an ice lolly, shaped like a rocket
A wry smile on his face, a twinkle in his eye
We had the best times, my Dad and I

1960's

WHAT DID WE DO WRONG?

There's rawness in your voice, you no longer whisper my name
No second chance for our romance, no playing the lovers game
Your hands no longer touch me, the eagerness has long gone
Leaving me to wonder...what did we do wrong?

Won't you tell me that I'm dreaming, and our love is still as strong?
Or will your honesty betray you, when you tell me you're moving on
We shared so many years together, built our castles in the sky
Chased rainbows and pipedreams, leaving me to wonder why...

I wish I could beg you to stay, but it's just not my style
Throw myself on your mercy, maybe you'll stay a little while
But like the last page in a book, or the final words in the song
All things come to a natural end...
we both did nothing wrong... nothing wrong.

WALKING AWAY

I'm trying so hard to let you go,
I put on a front, smile, say "Hello"
But in the cold light of day,
There's a longing in my heart.
I can't walk away...
Not been happy for a while,
Cheating on you is not my style
Nothing else for it I'd have to say
I'm leaving you, I'm walking away
I wasn't looking, but she saw me,
I saw her face, she looked so free
What would I do, what would I say,
I just knew I wouldn't walk away...
Woke this morning, she looked so sad,
Her eyes told our story, it felt so bad
I had to tell her, the right thing to do
Tell her I'm leaving, I'm in love with you.
Nothing else for it I'm going to day
My bags are packed...I'm walking away!

OUR JACK

I wonder what's going on, as you refuse to leave your bed.
Could it be your autism, and the chaos it creates in your head?
Or are you just being defiant because they're not playing into your hands
Refusing to go to school, perhaps you have other plans...
Or is it something quite different that seems to be worrying you
Are the words in your head too busy, and you don't know what to do?
I wonder what you feel like, as the pressure builds to the top
A multitude of teenage emotions "oh please *JUST STOP!*"
Are you struggling to make sense of this, so much has been going on?
Your life has changed forever, your childhoods been and gone
Or are you choosing to hide away from a world that's full of noise
You know you're safe in your bedroom, with your own rules and toys!
And it's here you have your Mario and the game of *your* choosing
A place to be on your own, always winning, never losing,
I may never have my answers jack, about what keeps you in your bed
And I can never feel like you do, because I'm not in your head
Yet, it doesn't affect our relationship because it's really clear to see
What jack and I share between us is normal for him and me.
He tells me about his day at school, and creates Lego for the shelf
He can tell me about his videos and the naughty Christmas elf
We share days out to theme parks where his body's as fast as his mind

He's always been so loving, and has treated me oh so kind
So what is societies answer, to special needs large or small?
Give them a collective label one size should fit all...
No there will be no defining label attached to my grandson's back
Because he is marvellously autistic and he is known lovingly as "Jack"

GRANDCHILDREN

If ever there's a time you cannot see or hear me – you'll know
I'm there
I'll be in the wind in the morning tugging at your hair.
I'll be in the sun at midday warming your skin
I'll be the light in the evening when darkness creeps in.
I'll support you and love you and watch as you grow,
And wait to embrace you when it's your time to go.

WOULD YOU CARE?

If I was to say that I loved you would you care?
If I said that I was leaving, would you despair?
If I placed my arms around you like a thickness of a coat
Would you slip into my lining and snuggle round my throat
If I said that I was leaving would you care?
Would you throw your arms around me stroke my hair
Or tell me that the thickness now feels thin
And throw away the coat and what had been...
If I said that I was leaving would you care?
Would you throw your hands and wave them in the air
Or tell me that our love will grow and grow...
If I said that I was leaving would you care?
The answer's no!

MRS MORRISS

Mrs Morriss sits alone, crocheting blankets, for faces
unknown.
A row of purple, a row of red, a row of pink, words left unsaid
Thoughts are random, procrastination has not set in
Like the tension of the yarn, she holds everything in.
She anchors the family she would never leave
Recycling her thoughts on her sleeve
So desperate to finish she works long into the night
Her reputation relies on it, praise is in sight.

DAD'S EMPTY CHAIR

Now you're not there it looks so enormous
Empty, some wide expanse of nothing
An epitaph to your final weeks of struggling
If you could manage to reach it then you were safe
Still in with a chance a chance that had long gone,
Like your youth, your strength, your character...
The carpet well worn, threadbare,
Where every day like some Hamster on a wheel
You'd use the same route guided by well fingered familiar
objects
Your pride and failing eyesight. The desire to survive.
The chair no longer waits ... it is empty

WHEN THE MUSIC STOPS

When the music stops, and the time has come, and there's
no one to keep you safe
When all seems lost and you bow your head
I will cover up your face
I will wipe your brow and kiss your feet and hold you tenderly
Then weep a thousand tears, as you say goodbye to me...
Learning to say goodbye, and let you go, is the hardest thing
I'll do
When the sun gives way to the moon, the day will be over,
over too soon.
You won't hear me crying, you won't see me fall, and you
won't feel the pain that will never stop at all...
I won't shed a tear, I won't let you down, I'll hold you till
your breath is cold and the music has no sound
You were my only lover, who shared my every move; there
will never be another to dance in the light of the moon.
It's all so unfair , there's no grey in your hair, and your body
longs to just dance, but the shadows draw near, and the end
that I fear seems only moments away...
You won't hear me crying, you won't see me fall, and you
won't feel the pain that will never stop at all...
I won't shed a tear, I won't let you down, I'll hold you till your
body's cold and the music has no sound...
I will wipe your brow and kiss your feet and hold you tenderly
Then weep a thousand tears, as you say goodbye to me...

COULD IT BE LOVE?

Save my soul and make me smile
Hold my hand for a while
Touch my body,
See I'm real
Bandage my scars
So I may heal.

I can't see it
Feel only its strength
It can't be measured by width or length
Indiscriminate sent from above
Winds uncontrollable
Could it be love?

FORBIDDEN LOVE

They never speak, they never smile
They hardly meet, once in a while.
They never touch, it's all too much
They're falling...
The love of theirs, will never be
They hide the pain, no one must see
Them falling....
A secret kept, what can they do
Forbidden love that grew and grew
Falling...
They didn't plan to feel this way
They said hello the other day...
Their eyes and hearts just fell in love
They've fallen...
They did not ask permission...
It was clearly more than this
Another new beginning...
It started with a kiss.

TOO LATE

It was too late now, as he lay so still
In his wax like body, far too ill
So she sat by his side, and cradled his hand
A worn out existence, one last stand.

She wondered could he hear her, the hearing's last to go
Although unspoken, she loved him so
Not a romantic love, the type born out of need
Two people thrown together, hoping to succeed...

She told him to stop it, he didn't deserve this death
But the words went unnoticed, they froze on her breath.
They had shared a lifetime together, brought up a family,
shared a home
And yet words went unspoken, two people together, yet alone.

1993

EXISTENCE

Most people enter this world with little or no possessions...
For those considered privileged, there may be money,
position...
Titles waiting to be claimed, shining halos and silver
spoons...
Platinum rings, classical music and hearts that sing to
unnamed tunes.
For the rest of us there are rusty chains and skies that rain,
misery and poverty...
The only thing that is certain, at the final curtain...
We all go out with nothing.

DEGENERATION

At the root of her body, where her soul should feed,
She's barren and withered, bereft of a seed.
Sad, sterile womb, redundant and cold,
No other reason, simply too old.
It was different once, thriving, alive
Like a ripe juicy fruit, too alive to die
But age can be cruel, unrelenting and cold
Like winter and frost, it kills the soul

IF ONLY

What is this... "If only"?
An excuse to blame
A reason to change
But would we...
Choose another path
Alter direction
Move on?
I doubt it!
A matter of choice
To use our voice
Think differently
Shout louder
What for?
To think... "if only"

CHARITY

What happened to me and trips to the sea?
When did I outgrow wanting to be free
Tomato sandwiches covered in sand,
Parents clutching my tiny hand
The opportunity to feel the sun
Margate beach here we come
Guillies buses, standing in line
Puffing and chugging
It's Pit holiday time

Trips to the sea, broke the monotony
Of a poor mining community
Mustn't waste trips to the sea,
Provided free, remain with me
Charity.

WHEN LOVE IS BROKEN

When love is broken and all that remains are
Memories of what was and can never be again
What do we do, do we leave our terrain
Or do we stand tall and expect another to go
Leave their home make the move we fear of
Or do we support each other to reach dry land
Begin another journey, hold each other's hand
Move forward into the unknown, grasp the nettle
Of opportunity and use it, to repair our broken wings
And fly to higher ground...

THE HOUSE ON THE HILL

There's a strong stench of liquor from the house on the hill,
From souls with broken bodies who linger there still.
Where did they come from guess nobody knows,
Each one has a story that will never be told
Walls without windows stare at faces without eyes
Never to be rescued, till the end of their lives
They've no dreams in their pockets, no money in their purse
 Just a sense of desperation and a never ending curse
They stare at each other, all seeing the same
Not expecting to be rescued from their unspoken pain.
What will become of them do they really care
About the house on the hill, no flowers grow there
What can be done for these suffering souls?
Who share silent screams and tears that don't flow,
Where's the compassion for the stories that tell,
Of the life that was stolen from the women in hell.
But wait now we see, someone's kicked down the door
And listened to the plight of what went before
Their stories have been told, someone took the time to care
For the unnamed women who wear flowers in their hair.

JOHN HARVEY

Most people know of Trafalgar the famous battle off 'The Cape',
Where Lord Nelson and his navy fought hard to decimate.
Deemed the greatest naval victory, defeated the enemy for sure,
Our Horatio is revered majestically, as though he lived next door!
He was a naval man of some substance, a real true intellect,
Defined as a national hero, one to cherish and respect.

However, take a moment, while I enlighten you,
To a hero buried in Eastry, who also commanded a crew.
The son of Richard and Elizabeth born in 1740 Eastry, Kent,
He entered the Navy in 54 where his future was hell-bent.
This was Captain John Harvey, reputed as honest and brave,
He has a statue to honour his courage, built securely in the Nave.

Educated in Calais, L'Ecole Royal de la Marine,
John Harvey was a true captain, a forceful sight to be seen.
His first ship was *The Falmouth*, at just fourteen years of age,
His naval career had started; he'd soon take centre stage.
From 59 till 62 his reputation was undeniably glowing,
Commissioned to a lieutenant his expertise truly showing.

Then, in 62 hostilities ceased and he found himself ashore,
Married Judith Wise from Sandwich, sons, she bore him four.
Daughters followed later, his family was complete,
His sons destined to be Admirals commanding their own fleet.
From 66 to 68 he commanded the sloop *Alarm*
His duty being to safeguard, protect the land from harm.

Many years were spent ashore, and this he couldn't alter,
Then in 78 to 80 excelled in *The Great Siege of Gibraltar*
Commanded the 60 gun *Panther* in the absence of Admiral Duff,
Distinguished himself as formidable, he was made of tough stuff.
This bravery did not go unnoticed; he spent a year with Sir Samuel Hood,
With his fleet in The West Indies, stood proud as only he could.

He returned to England in 82 after leaving the Island behind,
Instrumental in the war when to the *Sampson* he was assigned,
Distinguishing himself yet again he fought at *The Battle of The Cape*.
There seemed no end to the fighting, no risk too much to take.
Then in 83 another change, when he found himself post shore,
Never contemplating another fight aboard the *Arrogant 74*

But fight he did, on many fleets, became victorious out at sea,
Appointed to the ship *Magnificent* with Lord Howe in 93.
This command ended abruptly as Lord Howe recommissioned him to,
The ship known as *The Brunswick* at *The Battle of The First of June*.
The battle would prove bloody, preventing grain from reaching the French,
Many men lost their lives, there would be no pretence.

The Brunswick attacked so fiercely during *The Battle of the First of June*
It was proclaimed a valiant victory; it ended John's life too soon.
So next time you are looking for a hero, one to admire and recall,
Think of our own local John Harvey one of the most famous of them all.
For if it wasn't for this battle where he was injured beyond repair,
John Harvey would have made Admiral and with Nelson we should
compare.

LONELINESS

As I stare into the empty space,
I see thorns where once was lace.
Dullness creeps throughout my soul,
Unending, subtle, a gaping hole.
Nothing can fill this abys of dread,
like a butterfly it's elusive, enough said.

THE BIRTH OF A POEM

Eventually it finds me, and refuses to let go
Plants a seed in my head, a small embryo
It's there when I wake it's there when I sleep
Embedded in my life, does everything but speak!
I have no idea where it comes from it just suddenly appears
Like the bumble bee on my pillow, it buzzes in my ears
At times I try to ignore it, hoping it will go away
However, that's wishful thinking, my poem's here to stay.
It keeps playing with my senses, muddles and teases me
Keeps me guessing like a mother, of what the sex will be
It follows me into the shower; it bombards me when at work
It's selfish and relentless, my brains on full alert!
It never follows a genre; it may be modern, comic or plain
And if I fail to write it, it will never come again...
It doesn't develop immediately; it needs time to find its voice
I wonder what the message is; do I really have a choice?
So with pen in hand I brace myself and let the message flow
And watch the words come alive; they know just where to go!
A myriad of adjectives, verbs and common nouns
Sit alongside metaphors, as colourful as a clown
And now the birth is over my mind has clarity
I don't copyright the poem the poem copyrights me!

LOVE ON REFLECTION

At the time it seemed enough
Although now I know it wasn't
At the time I thought it would never end
But now I know differently
At the time I thought I would never overcome it
But now I know I can
There was a time when it preoccupied my life
But now things have changed
There was a time when I thought I would shrivel without it
But now I know your love was nothing more...
Than a handful of weeds.

WHEN NIGHT FALLS

When night falls and shutters the sky,
And beckons the storm to close its eye
Protecting us like thistle down
Draping us in velvet gown
We will sleep...
We will sleep...

FOR IVY AND PATRICK MORRISS

Oh to spend just a couple of hours
in the company of Mum and Dad
I have so much to tell them, what has happened
both good and bad
They could always make things better, with a word, or just a look
And that's why in their memory,
they're featured in my book...

DEAR MUM

Dear Mum,
There are so many reasons why I miss you...
The way you could make everything seem okay
Even though, it didn't always make it go away
Your complexity, love me don't leave me
The twinkle in your blue eyes, skin to die for
The way you had your say, rightly or wrongly
Your welsh cakes, your doughnuts, your voice
Well- worn hands smoothing down your apron
Chopping sticks to keep us warm, up before Dawn
The crocheting, the sewing, make do and mend
Your desire to survive, your family to defend
The hole in your pockets, that money fell through
Your welcome, your pride, it had cost you too
Your compassion, to a degree
Your expectations...usually of me
Your smile your warmth your oversized shawl
Your love for me and the family one and all
It's been seventeen years since you took your last breath
And I need you more today than the day you left.

Therapy

TIME HEALS

As the day races in to tomorrow, I'll leave today behind
I know it won't be easy, because it's always on my mind
The blow you dealt was deadly, like an arrow through the heart
The aftermath so damming, I don't know where to start...

Oh won't someone pick up the pieces, of a family, left shell
shocked
Put us back together, Join up the missing dots
Because we are broken, we are broken, like the eggshell on the
floor
Smashed in to tiny pieces, the damage done once more

I thought I'd seen the back of it, but the penny's here again
Causing havoc like no other, will we ever be free of the pain
I am tired of all this fighting, there is nothing more to say
Except time is a healer, so hurry, let's welcome today

DREAM TIME

In the middle of the night when everyone's asleep
To another world softly my thoughts and I creep
It's a special place where only I may go,
Familiar and comfortable I love it so

Sorrow, hatred, prejudice and sin
None of these dare enter in
I'm safe and happy surrounded with love
Protected and warm like a hand in a glove

I can float like a cloud or glide on a wing
Laugh, be happy, tap dance and sing
 I can see who I please talk with my Dad
Remember the fun, when alive, that we had

See my children as babes and hold them close
This instinctive emotion I miss the most
Play Netball and rounder's wear ribbons in my hair
Candy Floss and Coconuts taste the fun of the fair

I can breathe old emotions and savour the joy
See myself as a child, hug my favourite toy
Then all too soon, without any forewarning
I awake to the sound, of a new day dawning.

GUILT RIDDEN

Gingerly I step across a pond of frozen ice
How timid I feel, condemned, as poor as the mice
"What have I done?" I ask myself as I negotiate the crack
Emotions like the wind, sharp knives in my back
Stabbing on repeat, to ashamed to lift my head
Please leave me in peace and the safety of my bed

DEMENTIA

As I stroll down memory lane, nothing seems simple, it's not the same.
People and places, forgotten, unknown, confusion, anxiety,
I'm all alone.
How cruel is this illness that's confusing my mind,
Vascular Dementia, feels so unkind,
Stealing my present, erasing my past, memories are fading,
how long will they last?

Life seemed so easy, no trouble here, happiness, laughter,
nothing to fear.
What is happening? where is my home? my head is dizzy;
my baby's grown.
Who am I, think, I'm desperate to recall, the name of that person,
I don't know at all.
The photograph's not me, that women is old, I'm young and vibrant,
warm not cold.

Whatever's happening, I struggle to think, wait, I'm here,
I've found the link.
The malaise is lifting, my memory's retrieved, I'm lucid, aware,
oh! so relieved
Help is at hand, access is free, medication, and support,
all there for me.
I'm not alone, there are things I can do, join a club; make friends,
a trip or two.

Use aid memoirs, like "Turn off the water" techniques
to help me remember my daughter.
Turn off the electric, the gas, and the light,
keep my mobile charged, and clearly in sight.
Do puzzles and brain work, exercise and read,
the longer I stay active, the longer I'll breathe
So now I'm coping, I'm happy and whole, I feel empowered, alive;
I'm back in control!

OPTIMISM

When did spring surprise us?
With its enthusiastic smile
I nearly didn't see it
Took me a while
To rid myself of winter's chill
And the going of the old
Holding on to what's no more
Letting go of cold...
New beginnings are ahead ...
I just need to look
Further than the end of my nose
Get my head out of the book
Live my life, take risks
Say bring it on
For life is here for the taking
I just need to get along
Put myself right out there
Lift my head up to the sun
Say goodbye cold January
For your seasons had its run
Spring is on my shoulder
And if feels such a delight
At last the dark is over
For spring has turned on the light.

THE BENEFIT OF A CUPPA

Sharing a cuppa with a friend is like sharing your life
As you talk about the happiness, trouble and strife
A synchronised swallow is like sharing a smile
For it lifts and refreshes, at least for a while
You can chat about your past, make plans for the day
Feel the warmth of the cup, in a comforting way
Worries are shared, as we take time to listen
About the mosaic of life and all that might glisten
And when you are done and the cup runs dry
You will feel energised and watered and say...
"Goodbye"

CYCLE OF GRIEF

As I hit the ground I feel no pain
Nothing to lose nothing to gain
Just a mild concussion, easy to heal
Unlike the pain of feeling surreal
I pinch myself, there is no reaction
This angers me, I have no sanction
Just a gaping hole which remains unseen
Like memories, the wind the broken dream
Time heals I am told, more than I want to hear
For the grief is the only thing which keeps you near
Without pain and anguish and feeling alone
I know I will have accepted the loss and cracked the stone
And when this happens, people say I will live again
Throw off this coat that stops the rain
Feel the sun again and breathe lighter air
Give myself permission to live if only I dare

LIVE THE DAY

When the actions of others are questioned, and we spring to
their defence
When core beliefs are tested and nothing in our life makes sense
When the world we know seems different, and will never be the
same
We can hold our head up high, and choose not to play the game

We can learn to think quite differently, reframe and challenge
our mind
Replace rejection and loss with harmony, and then we just
might find
The peace we all keep looking for, is still within our reach
And everyone can breathe again and feel the sweet relief

We can turn our head to the sunshine; we can end the endless
strife
We can stop the daily challenge, and shake off the pain that's
rife
We can learn to be accepting, of others and their ways
Fill our lives with simple compassion and learn to live the day.

BAN THE BULLY

A wolf in sheep's clothing, is a saying often heard,
As they appear placid and humble, until the victim's lured.
You find the bully everywhere, in school, at home in work,
In fact there's not a single place, where the bully does not lurk!

They choose their victim carefully like a bird hunting their prey,
To feed their insecurities, they inflict throughout the day.
The victim feels so helpless, unworthy and alone,
If only they'd find the courage to use a helpline phone.

There are people, who will listen and help them just to see,
There's no need to suffer in silence; the help is there and free.
Support can make the difference; inform them of their rights,
To banish the bully forever, and end the soul destroying fights...

MOMENTS

In those unguarded moments, when the sun goes down
And no warmth can be felt, from the unfamiliar ground
You will find her waiting for time to allow
The opportunity to be alone in the familiar "Now"

NOSTALGIC MOMENT

When time has flown from my life,
Like the chick leaving the comfort of the nest,
I will not bemoan or anxiously stress.
For as with every beginning,
There comes a natural end,
And as the chick learns to fly,
I must learn to ascend.

RIGHTS AND CHOICES

You have the right to choose
And to choose is your right
The right to choose is valuable
So hold it very tight.

Independence
You have something very special
Which is very, very nice?
It's known as independence
Its value, beyond a price

THE BEST VERSION OF YOU

Hoe through your heart and pull out all weeds,
Deadly and dangerous, poisonous seeds
Cut out the hate, it destroys and maims,
Pollinate the love, plant healthy grains.

Nurture positive thoughts, grow them in piles,
Then harvest in abundance, a sack of smiles.
Dig out expectations, they ruin the terrain,
Stock up on laughter and count up the gains!

A garden to be proud of that's empathic and fair
Borne from your compassion that now grows there
A heart full of sunshine, a healthy head too
Just for creating the best version of you!

GUILTY FEELINGS

In the depths of despair, lays a monster so deep
With an overgrown nose, and a secret to keep
Huge and menacing, it aims to appal
Like the volcano it waits, to swallow us all!

It shows us no mercy, when it rears its head
Recoil never; there is tears to shed!
Like a pin to a balloon, it's powerful and strong
Inappropriately we feed it, nourish it along.

Automatic and negative, dark thoughts we choose
To self-blame, self- sabotage and eventually lose.
Only satisfied and content, when our strength is low,
Taking us to a place, where we need not go…

But wait, consider this, thoughts can be changed,
From negative to positive if you just rearrange…
Change the narrative, choose your own story
Lift your head high and celebrate the glory!

Say "bring it on," and banish the strife…
Take the power from guilt and live your life…
You have only one so don't think meek
Think complex, fallible and oh so unique!

Seasons

CHANGING SEASONS

The Autumnal hues of yellow serene,
Mingle with summer's fading green
Winter waits with frozen face
Whilst spring basks idyllically, last in the race.

SPRING COMETH

It's here again the season called spring
With its aromatic flowers and birds that sing
A chorus of thanks now winter's done
Nests can be built, in the warmth of the sun
A time for new beginnings, bestowed from above
Spring cometh, at last, bringing hope and love
A time free from Covid and its deadly rampage
Savage, unrelenting indiscriminate of age
You've done your worse, now leave the scene
Your time is up, we have the vaccine.

THE GARDEN OF YEW TREE CLOSE

White Ovum Lillie's standing proud and tall,
Over-shadow the violets so delicate and small.
Purple pansies, lilac and vine,
Cling to the warmth of Summer time.
The colours of nature so melodic and bright,
Dread the cold of winter's blight.
Soaking up the rain and drying in the breeze,
Avoiding the inevitable Artic freeze.

MOTHER NATURE

Have you ever compared Mother Nature, against the efforts
of the great?
Who hang in famous galleries the Louvre or the Tate?
Displayed in all their glory, no finer sight you'll see,
A Grassie or Da Vinci, the sneaky Banksy.

Painted to perfection, a name of their own
Revered for their talent, styles well known!
Fine Art, Renaissance, and Street Art too
A feast for the eyes, undeniably true

However, take a moment, cast your eyes and see
Mother Nature with her palate a style known as "Free"
A tapestry of colours, dancing in the rain
Refreshing the dusty hedgerows, time and time again

The brightness of the moonlight, the crisp cold morn
The setting of the sunset, the bright new Dawn
She paints the world continually, will never make a fuss
And unlike famous artistes, Mother Nature needs no brush.

DEAR FAMILY AND FRIENDS

When it's my turn to go, share the good things, not the bad
Laugh at the funny things I said, forget the sad
Paint me in a good light, cut me some slack
For anyone who knows me knows I'll be back
Play happy music, remember me through song
Dance be colourful, do a sing a long
Lift up your heart, celebrate the day
Think of the time, when I'll come and stay
For I will always be with you, just wait and see
The white feather you'll find will be sent from me!

Hope you enjoyed the book
Love as Always Lin xx

Lightning Source UK Ltd.
Milton Keynes UK
UKHW010833201021
392527UK00003B/407